MW00899131

This book belongs to:

_____

About This Book

Christmas Around the World invites young readers to explore 21 enchanting stories, each one revealing unique Christmas traditions from different countries. Through the adventures of children across the globe, this book shares the joy, kindness, and togetherness that make the holiday season so magical.

In every story, readers will learn about special customs, from lantern festivals to caroling, Christmas feasts, and festive games, and discover how different cultures celebrate in their own way. More than just tales, these stories remind us that the spirit of Christmas is universal, filled with warmth, wonder, and the joy of sharing with family and friends. Perfect for young explorers eager to see the world through the lens of Christmas traditions, this book offers a beautiful journey through the magic of the season.

Mexico

"The Las Posadas Celebration and the Magical Piñata"

Lucia, a brave 8-year-old girl, and her friends join the Las Posadas procession, a traditional Mexican celebration that symbolizes Mary and Joseph's search for shelter. With each stop, the children sing and knock on doors, asking for shelter just like Mary and Joseph did. Laughter and music fill the air, and as they move along, the excitement builds. On a magical December evening, they finally reach the last house, where a brightly colored piñata awaits them. Each child takes turns swinging eagerly, and instead of just candy, the piñata releases tiny toys and ornaments, each with an old story about Mexican Christmas traditions.

Lucia listens with wonder to tales of kindness, hospitality, and giving. One of the tiny toys, a little figurine of Mary, reminds her of the importance of family and supporting one another. Another story speaks of children sharing treats with those in need. As she absorbs these lessons, Lucia feels a special warmth, realizing that the joy of Christmas grows when we share our gifts with others. She heads home with a heart full of gratitude, knowing that the true magic of Christmas is found in generosity and celebrating together with family and friends.

Norway
"The Search for Julenissen"

In a small, snow-covered Norwegian village, Erik, a curious 9-year-old boy is filled with excitement as he learns about Julenissen, the gnome-like figure who brings gifts to children on Christmas Eve. During his holiday visit to his grandmother's cozy cottage, she tells him a magical story: Julenissen lives deep in the forest nearby, and only children with pure hearts who truly believe can find him. Erik's eyes light up with wonder, and he decides he must try to find Julenissen himself.

Bundled in warm clothes, Erik sets off into the forest the next morning, his boots crunching in the crisp snow, and his breath forming little clouds in the cold air. He peers around every tree, looks under snow-covered bushes, and listens to the quiet songs of the birds, hoping for a glimpse of the Christmas gnome. The deeper he goes, the quieter the forest becomes, until all he hears is the soft fall of snowflakes.

Just as he begins to think it might only be a story, Erik spots tiny footprints in the snow, leading to a small pouch nestled beneath a tree. Inside, he finds a handful of gingerbread cookies and a little note that reads, "For those who believe." With a heart full of joy, Erik heads back home, realizing that the true magic of Christmas lies in faith, hope, and the simple wonders around him.

Philippines
"The Lights of Parol"

Mateo, an 8-year-old boy lives in a small village in the Philippines where Christmas is celebrated with a beautiful Festival of Lights called the "Parol Festival." Every December, families gather to make parols—star-shaped lanterns that symbolize the Star of Bethlehem, illuminating the village in colorful lights. Mateo is determined to create the most beautiful parol to honor his family's tradition, but he quickly finds himself struggling. No matter how hard he tries, his parol doesn't look as bright and unique as he'd imagined.

Frustrated, Mateo is ready to give up, but his younger brother offers to help. Together, they gather materials around the village and come up with the idea to decorate the parol with dried palm leaves and vibrant hibiscus flowers, adding a touch of natural beauty. Carefully, they weave the leaves and flowers around the frame, and, little by little, the parol takes on a unique glow, unlike any other in the village.

On the night of the festival, the village is filled with parols, each one more radiant than the last. But when Mateo's parol is lit, it stands out with its simple yet striking beauty, catching the attention of everyone around. The villagers admire his creativity and teamwork with his brother, and Mateo realizes that sometimes the best ideas come when we share and work together. As his family gathers around him, he feels proud to have created something that brings joy to others, understanding that Christmas magic shines brightest when shared with loved ones.

Italy

"Befana's Little Helper"

In Italy, children eagerly await the arrival of Befana, a magical old woman who brings gifts and sweets on the night of January 5th, the Eve of Epiphany. Sofia, a brave 7-year-old girl curious to know how this "magical grandmother" looks, leaves a cookie and a glass of milk by the window, hoping to lure Befana in. Determined to stay awake, she watches the stars from her bedroom window, but eventually, her eyelids grow heavy, and she falls asleep.

In the middle of the night, Sofia is startled awake by a soft rustling sound outside her window. Peeking out, she catches a glimpse of Befana, with her broom and her tattered sack, moving quietly through the night. But as Befana adjusts her sack, a few candies and treats spill onto the ground! Without thinking, Sofia grabs her slippers and rushes outside, tiptoeing over the cold cobblestone. With a shy smile, she offers to help Befana gather the scattered treats. Befana's eyes twinkle with warmth, and together, they place each candy back in the sack. Before flying off, Befana gives Sofia a small gift and a wink, saying, "Thank you for your kindness, little one." As Sofia returns to her cozy bed, she realizes that the real magic of the season isn't just in gifts but in helping and sharing with others. That night, she falls asleep with a heart full of warmth and a lesson she'll always remember.

Japan
"The Christmas Cake Celebration"

In Japan, Christmas is celebrated as a time of friendship and joy, and Hana's family has a tradition of making a special Christmas cake covered with whipped cream and topped with strawberries. This year, Hana decides she wants to surprise her family by making the cake herself. Excited but nervous, she begins to mix the ingredients but quickly realizes that baking is harder than it seems. The batter turns out lumpy, and the cream isn't as fluffy as she'd hoped.

Seeing her struggle, Hana's mother and father step in to help, guiding her with patience. Together, they laugh, fix the batter, and find ways to make the whipped cream just right. Hana decides to add an extra-special touch by hiding a layer of chocolate in the middle of the cake as a secret surprise. Carefully, they spread the chocolate, then finish decorating with strawberries and a dusting of powdered sugar.

That evening, when they finally cut into the cake, her family is thrilled by the unexpected chocolate layer. As they enjoy each bite, Hana feels a deep happiness in seeing their delight. She realizes that the most meaningful memories come not just from the finished cake, but from working together and sharing joy with her family. The Christmas cake becomes more than a treat—it's a symbol of the love and laughter they share, a reminder of the special moments that make the holiday magical.

Finland
"A Letter to Joulupukki"

In Finland, children eagerly write letters to Joulupukki, the Finnish Santa Claus, who lives in the snowy forests of Lapland. This year, Mika, a 9-year-old boy, and his younger sister Elina decided to write a different kind of letter. Rather than asking for gifts, they want to thank Joulupukki for the joy he brings to the holiday season. Together, they sit by the warm glow of the fire, recalling their favorite winter memories. In the letter, they tell Joulupukki about decorating the Christmas tree with their parents, making snow angels in the yard, and the cozy evenings they spend reading stories. Once their letter is finished, they carefully seal it and bundle it up in warm scarves and mittens to brave the chilly evening air. As they walk through the snowy village, they feel the excitement building, knowing they're sending something truly special. When they reach the special postbox meant for letters to Joulupukki, they slip the letter inside. Just as they're about to leave, they notice a small scroll tied with a red ribbon resting on the box.

Curiously, they open it to find a message written in elegant script: "Thank you, Mika and Elina, for sharing the Christmas spirit. Wishing you a magical holiday season! – Joulupukki's Elves." The siblings smile, feeling a warmth that has nothing to do with their winter coats. Mika and Elina realize that even a small gesture of gratitude can make the holiday season feel magical and that the spirit of Christmas shines brightest through acts of kindness and thanks.

Netherlands
"Shoes for Sinterklaas"

In the Netherlands, children leave their shoes by the door for Sinterklaas, who arrives on December 5th with treats and small gifts. This year, Lars a curious 8-year-old boy is especially excited to take part in the tradition. Wanting to make a memorable impression, he decides to leave not just his shoes but also a hand-drawn letter filled with colorful pictures of his favorite holiday moments. With Max by his side, Lars carefully places his shoes by the door, imagining Sinterklaas's delight when he sees the surprise.

The next morning, Lars rushes to his shoes, eager to see if Sinterklaas visited. To his amazement, he finds a unique toy nestled inside, along with a small scroll. Unrolling it, he reads a message from Sinterklaas himself, praising Lars's creativity and his generous spirit in sharing gifts with his younger brother. Overjoyed, Lars realizes that Sinterklaas saw not only his gift but also his thoughtfulness.

As Lars admires his new toy, he understands that Christmas joy doesn't come from the gifts themselves, but from the small acts of kindness and the simple joys shared with others. Smiling, he decides to make Sinterklaas a tradition of sharing and creativity, knowing it's these moments that make the holiday season truly magical.

Greece
"The Dance of the Kalikantzaroi"

In Greece, there's a legend about the Kalikantzaroi—mischievous goblins who appear during Christmas to play harmless pranks. Nikos, a curious young boy, hears tales of these playful creatures from his grandmother and becomes determined to catch a glimpse of them himself. On Christmas Eve, with the family gathered around the table for a festive meal, Nikos and his cousins keep a close watch, hoping the Kalikantzaroi will make an appearance.

Later that night, when the house is quiet, Nikos spots small tracks of dust on the floor and tangled garlands draped over chairs. He nudges his cousins, and together they laugh, imagining the goblins tiptoeing around, playing tricks while everyone sleeps. Instead of being upset, the children decide to leave little "gifts" for the Kalikantzaroi—crumbs from cookies and shiny ribbons. As they giggle and swap stories about the goblins, Nikos realizes that the true magic of Christmas is not in the decorations or gifts, but in the unexpected joys and surprises that come with it. This year, his holiday memories are filled with laughter, mischief, and the wonder of Kalikantzaroi's playful visit.

Brazil

"Christmas Angels on the Night of Estrelas"

In Brazil, Christmas is celebrated with lights and stars that fill the skies. Ana, an 8-year-old girl is spending her Christmas at her grandmother's home, where she learns about the tradition of "Noite das Estrelas" (Night of the Stars). Her grandmother explains that on this special night, people light lanterns and place candles to honor the Christmas angels, who bring blessings to those who believe. Eager to join in, Ana carefully prepares her lantern, with her grandmother guiding her.

On Christmas night, Ana lights her lantern and whispers a secret wish, hoping the angels will hear her. As she looks up at the night sky, filled with the glow of lanterns and stars, she feels a special kind of magic. Just before midnight, a shooting star streaks across the sky, and her grandmother gently tells her that the angels have received her wish.

Ana realizes that Christmas is not only about gifts and celebrations but also about hope and believing in the magic of wishes. Her heart fills with warmth, knowing that sometimes, the most precious gifts are those that bring faith and joy.

Poland
"The Dinner of Twelve Dishes"

In Poland, Christmas Eve is marked by a special dinner of twelve dishes, each representing one of the twelve apostles. This year, Kasia a 9-year-old girl is filled with excitement as she joins her family in preparing the feast. Every family member contributes a unique dish, and Kasia's job is to set the table and place an extra plate for the "unexpected guest"—a beloved tradition symbolizing kindness and hospitality for those who may need it.

Before dinner begins, they gather to break oplatek, a thin, blessed wafer, and share wishes of health and happiness for the coming year. As the meal unfolds, each dish carries a story. Kasia listens as her parents and grandparents recount their fondest memories, lessons they've learned, and dreams for the future. The first dish brings tales of perseverance; the next, a story of kindness from her grandmother's youth.

The warm glow of candlelight fills the room as laughter and stories flow with each course, from mushroom soup to sweet poppy seed rolls. Kasia realizes that each dish, no matter how simple, represents the shared love and memories of her family. By the end of the meal, her heart is full of gratitude, and she understands that the true magic of Christmas lies in these moments of togetherness and tradition.

Russia
"Babushka's Evening"

In Russia, Christmas is celebrated on January 7th, and children hear stories of Babushka, a kind old woman who travels through villages, bringing gifts to those with kind hearts. On a chilly winter evening, Sasha, an 8-year-old girl, and her friend Katya decide to put on a small performance of carols and poems at Sasha's family home, hoping that Babushka might hear their voices and visit them.

They sing with all their hearts, filling the house with warmth and laughter, as family members gather to watch and clap. When the evening ends, the girls step outside for fresh air, and there, on the doorstep, they find a small, traditional Matryoshka doll left just for them—a symbol of good luck and kindness. Sasha feels a rush of joy and gratitude, understanding that the true gifts of Christmas lie in the traditions and stories that bring people together.

That night, Sasha learns that sharing these special customs brings happiness not only to others but to herself as well. The memory of Babushka's visit and the Matryoshka doll becomes a precious reminder that stories and traditions are treasures to be cherished and shared.

Australia

"Christmas on the Beach"

In Australia, Christmas arrives in the middle of summer, and many families choose to celebrate on the beach. This year, Liam a 7-year-old boy is excited to plan a unique Christmas with his parents and little sister. They set off for a sunny day by the sea, packing a picnic and decorations in their bags. Once there, they begin collecting seashells and small stones to create a Christmas tree in the sand, decorating it with colorful ribbons and shells they find along the shore.

After building their "sand tree," they play a friendly game of cricket, a beloved Australian Christmas tradition. Laughter fills the air as Liam and his sister run across the warm sand, feeling the ocean breeze. Once the game ends, the family gathers around their sandy Christmas tree, sharing small gifts and snapping photos to remember the day. Liam realizes how special this warm, sunny Christmas feels, even without snow or a fir tree.

As they watch the waves roll in, he understands that Christmas magic can be found wherever the family is—whether on a snowy winter's day or a bright, sunlit beach. The joy of the season, he learns, is in being together and creating new memories.

Germany
"The Advent Calendar of Surprises"

In Germany, children eagerly count down the days to Christmas by opening a door on their Advent calendar each morning and discovering a small treat or surprise inside. This year, Leni an 8-year-old girl, and her brother, Max are especially excited, as their mother has crafted a special Advent calendar just for them. Each door holds not only sweets but also a unique note with a surprise activity.

One morning, they open the door to find a tiny map of their neighborhood and a note that reads, "Bring joy to others today." Curious, Leni and Max follow the map, setting out on a journey of kindness. They help carry groceries for Mrs. Fischer, their elderly neighbor, clear snow from the walkway of Mr. Krause, and deliver handmade holiday cards to families nearby. With each task, they see the joy they're bringing to others, and the smiles they receive fill their hearts with warmth.

As the Advent days pass, Leni and Max look forward to each morning's surprise, eager to see what new kindness awaits them. By Christmas Eve, they've shared countless small acts of joy throughout the neighborhood, and they realize that the true magic of the season isn't found in receiving gifts but in the happiness they can spread. Their Advent calendar has taught them that the Christmas spirit shines brightest when shared.

Iceland

"The Visit of the Thirteen Yule Lads"

In Iceland, children ea, a 9-year-old boyerly await the arrival of the Yule Lads. These thirteen mischievous brothers visit each night, starting on December 12th, leaving small gifts or surprises in the shoes left on the windowsill. Eirikur and his friends are fascinated by these magical visitors and decide to stay up one night, hoping to catch a glimpse of a Yule Lad in action.

As the night goes on, they wait quietly by the window, eyes wide with anticipation. Eventually, they spot tiny footprints near the windowsill and find a small message tucked inside one of the shoes. The note, left by one of the Yule Lads, encourages them to be kind, and cheerful, and to spread joy throughout the season. Filled with excitement and wonder, Eirikur realizes that the mystery and traditions of Christmas bring a unique happiness to the holiday.

In the days that follow, Eirikur shares the note's message with his friends, and together, they embrace the spirit of the Yule Lads by sharing small acts of kindness. He learns that it's these little surprises and moments of magic that make Christmas truly special, leaving memories to treasure year after year.

England
"The Carol Singers' Night"

Christmas caroling is a cherished tradition in England, with children going door to door singing for their neighbors. This year, Oliver an 8-year-old boy and his younger sister Emily join the village group of carolers, but Oliver feels a bit shy about singing in front of everyone. As they go from house to house, their voices fill the chilly night air, and neighbors greet them warmly with cookies and hot chocolate, which helps Oliver relax and find his voice.

With each song, Oliver feels a little braver, encouraged by the smiles and cheers from the people they meet. The carolers are eventually invited to sing in the village square, where a small crowd gathers to listen. Standing in front of everyone, Oliver takes a deep breath, and his voice blends with the others, strong and confident.

As the carolers finish their last song and the crowd applauds Oliver realizes that sometimes, all it takes is a little courage to spread joy. He feels proud and happy, learning that sharing Christmas cheer can bring people together and make the season brighter.

France
"The Bûche de Noël Cake"

In France, the traditional Christmas dessert is the Bûche de Noël, a chocolate roll cake shaped like a yule log. This year, Chloé a 9-year-old girl is spending Christmas with her grandmother, who teaches her how to make this special dessert. Together, they carefully prepare the cake, decorating it with small mint sprigs and a dusting of powdered sugar to resemble freshly fallen snow.

As they work, Chloé's grandmother shares the story behind the yule log tradition, explaining how families in the old days would burn a large log in the hearth to bring warmth and good fortune to the home. Listening to her grandmother's tales, Chloé realizes that holiday recipes carry not only delightful flavors but also pieces of history and magic.

That evening at dinner, as everyone enjoys the beautifully decorated Bûche de Noël, Chloé feels a special connection to the past. She learns that these culinary traditions add a deeper warmth to the season, enriching their celebrations with cherished stories and memories passed down through generations.

Romania
"The Star of Christmas Eve"

In Romania, children celebrate Christmas Eve by carrying a brightly decorated star from house to house, singing carols to announce the birth of Jesus. This year, Andrei, an 8-year-old boy, and his cousin Ioana decide to take part in this beloved tradition. Together with Andrei's father, they work hard to create a beautiful star, decorating it with colorful paper and little bells that jingle as they walk.

As they begin their journey through the village, Andrei feels nervous, but Ioana's cheerful encouragement helps him find his courage. In each home they visit, people welcome them warmly, offering fruits, pastries, and walnuts as thanks for their songs. With every house, Andrei's confidence grows, and he feels the warmth and happiness of sharing this tradition with others.

By the end of the evening, Andrei realizes how special it is to keep alive a tradition that brings joy and unites the community. He learns that customs like this are more than just celebrations—they are a bridge that connects hearts and fills the season with meaning and togetherness.

Sweden
"The Feast of Saint Lucia"

In Sweden, on December 13th, Saint Lucia's Day is celebrated, symbolizing light amid winter. Elin, an 8-year-old girl is chosen to be Saint Lucia at her school, wearing a crown of candles and offering traditional saffron buns called lussekatter to her classmates. She feels excited but also a bit nervous about her important role. Sensing this, her mother tells her the story of Saint Lucia, who brought light and hope during the darkest days of the year.

Encouraged by her mother's words, Elin embraces her role with confidence. As she leads the procession, singing songs and sharing the saffron buns, she feels proud to bring a touch of brightness to her friends and family. Elin learns that sometimes, a small act of kindness can illuminate an entire day and that she, too, can be a bearer of light and hope.

Portugal

"The Table for Those Who Have Passed"

In Portugal, on Christmas Eve, families prepare a special table with an extra place setting to honor loved ones who have passed away. This year, Sofia, an 8-year-old girl is curious about the tradition, and she joins her grandmother in preparing the table, asking about the family members who are no longer with them. As they set out the dishes and decorations, her grandmother shares memories of her father, who loved singing carols and filling the house with laughter.

As Sofia listens, she feels a warm sense of closeness to the people her grandmother remembers so fondly. She realizes that even though these family members aren't physically present, their love and memories continue to surround them. By the end of the evening, Sofia understands that Christmas is not only about those gathered around the table but also about the loved ones they carry in their hearts. She learns that true family ties are never broken, and this tradition keeps those memories alive, filling the holiday with warmth and connection.

Austria
"The Lights of Advent"

In Austria, the Advent season is celebrated with the tradition of lighting candles on an Advent wreath, with four candles—one for each Sunday leading up to Christmas. Felix an 8-year-old boy and his sister, Anna, are excited to help their family prepare the Advent wreath, decorating it with pine branches, red ribbons, and pinecones.

Each Sunday, their family gathers to light a new candle, and their grandmother shares a Christmas story. As the candles burn, Felix feels a special peace and learns that each candle represents hope, peace, joy, and love. On the final Sunday, all four candles glow brightly, filling the room with warmth, and Felix realizes that Advent is not just about waiting for gifts but also a time for reflection and gratitude.

Felix understands that Christmas traditions like the Advent wreath bring family and friends together, filling their hearts and homes with light and preparing them for the spirit of the holidays.

China
"The Lantern Festival of the New Year"

In China, the winter holiday season ends with the Lantern Festival, celebrated at the close of the Lunar New Year, when people send their wishes into the sky for the coming year. Ming a 9-year-old boy and his friend Wei are excited to create their lanterns, decorating them with drawings and writing down hopes for peace, health, and friendship.

On the night of the Festival, the two friends join their families and neighbors in a local park, where everyone releases their lanterns, which slowly rise, lighting up the night sky. As they watch the lanterns float higher, Ming feels a deep joy and learns that traditions not only bring people together but also give them hope and courage for the future.

Through this experience, Ming discovers that the Lantern Festival is more than just a beautiful display of lights; it's a way to share dreams and wishes with loved ones, bringing in the new year with optimism and unity.

Thank you

To all the young adventurers and families who have traveled with us across the globe in these pages, thank you for joining this journey of wonder and tradition. Christmas is celebrated in countless unique ways around the world, and it's our hope that these stories have brought a touch of that magic into your heart and home. From the joyful sounds of carols to the warmth of family gatherings, each tradition shared here is a gift from cultures near and far, filled with joy, kindness, and togetherness.

A heartfelt thank you to every reader, parent, and child for keeping the spirit of Christmas alive and celebrating the beauty of our shared world. May these stories inspire you to cherish your own traditions and explore new ones with those you love.

Wishing you peace, joy, and endless wonder this Christmas and always.

Stefany Snee

Made in United States
Troutdale, OR
12/11/2024

26329463R00031